Simply Science

FLIGHT

Discover Science Through Facts and Fun

By Gerry Bailey

Science and curriculum consultant:

Debra Voege, M.A., science curriculum resource teacher

Gareth Stevens Publishing

Please visit our web site at www.garethstevens.com.
For a free catalog describing our list of high-quality books, call 1-800-542-2595 (USA)
or 1-800-387-3178 (Canada). Our fax: 1-877-542-2596

Library of Congress Cataloging-in-Publication Data
Bailey, Gerry.
      Flight / by Gerry Bailey.
         p. cm.—(Simply Science)
      Includes bibliographical references and index.
      ISBN-10: 1-4339-0032-7   ISBN-13: 978-1-4339-0032-7 (lib. bdg.)
      1. Flight—Juvenile literature. 2. Aeronautics—Juvenile literature. I. Title.
   TL547.B323 2009
   629.13—dc22   2008027569

This North American edition first published in 2009 by
Gareth Stevens Publishing
A Weekly Reader® Company
1 Reader's Digest Road
Pleasantville, NY 10570-7000 USA

This U.S. edition copyright © 2009 by Gareth Stevens, Inc. Original edition copyright © 2008 by
Diverta Publishing, First published in Great Britain in 2008 by Diverta Publishing Ltd, London.

Gareth Stevens Executive Managing Editor: Lisa M. Herrington
Gareth Stevens Creative Director: Lisa Donovan
Gareth Stevens Designer: Keith Plechaty
Gareth Stevens Associate Editor: Amanda Hudson
Publisher: Keith Garton
Special thanks to Jessica Cohn

Photo Credits: Cover (tc) Tim Jenner/Shutterstock Inc., (bl) Chris H. Galbraith/Shutterstock Inc.; pp. 4–5 Michael
Rolands/Shutterstock Inc.; p. 6 (c) JoLin/Shutterstock Inc., (b) NASA/GSFC; p. 8 Topfoto; p. 9 (t) Manoir du Clos Lucz/Dagli
Orti/The Art Archive, (b) Mary Evans Picture Library/Alamy; p. 11 Petros Tsonis/Shutterstock Inc.; p. 15 (t)
Kristian/Shutterstock Inc., (br) Tim Zurowski/Shutterstock Inc.; p. 17 Karen Hadley/Shutterstock Inc.; p. 20 (t) Adrian
Steele/Shutterstock Inc., (b) Roger Violet/Topfoto; p. 21 Tim Jenner/Shutterstock Inc.; p. 23 Foster/The Flight Collection;
p. 25 NASA; p. 26 (t) Mark Bond/Shutterstock Inc., (c) Richard A. McGuirk/Shutterstock Inc., (b) Graham
Taylor/Shutterstock Inc.; p. 27 (t) Anson Hung/Shutterstock Inc., (c) Roger Violet/Topfoto, (b) Topfoto; p. 28 (tr) Chris H.
Galbraith/Shutterstock Inc., (bl) Popperfoto/Alamy; p. 29 (t) Joel Bauchat Grant/Shutterstock Inc., (b) Tomasz
Gulla/Shutterstock Inc.

Illustrations: Steve Boulter and Xact Studio

Diagrams: Karen Radford

Every effort has been made to trace the copyright holders for the photos used in this book, and the publisher
apologizes in advance for any unintentional omissions. We would be pleased to insert the appropriate
acknowledgements in any subsequent edition of this publication.

Printed in the United States of America

1 2 3 4 5 6 7 8 9 13 12 11 10 09

Simply Science
FLIGHT

CONTENTS

What Is Flight?

Flight is movement through the air. Most birds and insects can fly. People saw these animals in the air and wanted to be able to take flight, too.

People don't have wings, so we need help to fly. That's where inventions such as the kite, hot air balloon, **glider**, and airplane come in. They made human flight possible.

So let's fly a kite

or fly in an airplane

or ride in a hot air balloon.

Let's soar in a rocket.

Balloons are filled with hot air in preparation for flight.

The Kite

One of the first things people flew were kites. Kites have been around for a long time. They were invented in China more than 2,000 years ago!

A kite is a kind of aircraft. Usually it's made of something lightweight, such as cloth or paper that's stretched over a frame. It's flown, or controlled, from the ground by a long cord.

Message on the Wind

1. Long ago, soldiers didn't have aircraft to help them scout out the size of an enemy army. They had to use their eyesight, which meant getting dangerously close.

2. Spies had to gather information and carry it back to camp. If the enemy was in the way, the spies had to sneak through enemy ranks.

I don't like the idea of that!

Wind Power

Kites use wind energy for power. Wind energy can also be used to power sailboats and wind surfers.

3. Spies could tape messages to birds and hope the birds flew the right way.

4. Or they could wave flags to send messages. That did not work if hills and trees were in the way, though. Then soldiers thought of sending messages through the air another way.

5. They made cross-shaped frames with cloth stretched from end to end. These simple kites could catch the wind and carry messages. The kites could be controlled by long cords.

Air Pressure

Air pushes kites around. It can push people, too. When we jump up, we can't jump very far. That is, in part, because air is pressing down. Air is pushing back.

When you look up in the air you usually don't see much—perhaps the odd bird or a cloud or plane. That doesn't mean there's nothing there.

The air is part of a layer of gases called the atmosphere. The atmosphere wraps around Earth like a blanket. It helps keep us warm and protects us from the heat and harmful rays of the Sun. When the air moves, we call it wind. You can feel air when it is moving.

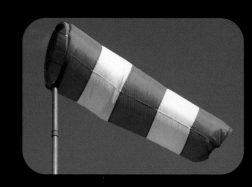

A windsock fills with air and shows the direction in which the wind is blowing.

What Is Air Pressure?

The atmosphere is heavy and presses down on us. This pressure is called air pressure. The further up we go in the atmosphere, the less air presses down. There is less air pressure on a mountain. Less air means less oxygen, too, and humans need oxygen to breathe.

15% oxygen in air

Air is made up of molecules of different gases. At sea level, oxygen **molecules** take up about 21 percent of air. High on a mountain, there is less—about 15 percent of that air is oxygen. Many people find it difficult to breathe easily high in the air.

21% oxygen in air

Light Things Can Float

We used to think we were too heavy for flight. Then we realized that studying the shape of birds' wings might help us figure out a way to fly.

We thought about balloons filled with air.

Could we fly like birds or balloons?

How Wings Work

People watched birds fly and wanted wings of their own. The special shape of a bird's wings allows the animal to fly.

Wing Shape

A wing is curved and **streamlined**. In the air, a wing divides airflow into two flows, one traveling under the wing and one going over the top. The one on top moves faster.

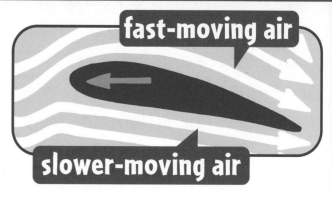

The fast-moving air on top pulls on the air above it and takes it downward. The faster air moves, the less air pressure there is. So the air pressure above a wing is lower than below the wing. The air, the angle of the wing, and air pressure differences around the wing create lift.

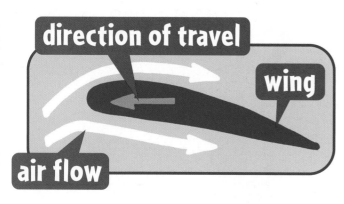

The two flows of air move differently. That difference helps lift the wing.

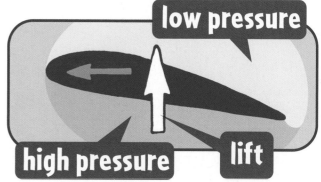

The higher air pressure below pushes the wing up.

The wings of soaring birds, like this eagle, inspired people to design flying machines.

low pressure

On a plane, the wings act like a huge scoop. As they scoop, or pull air down, the air pressure becomes lower above the wing. That helps the plane rise.

A Hovering Bird

Hummingbirds can **hover** by rotating their wings in a very fast figure-eight motion. Some species can beat their wings up to 80 times a second!

Leonardo's Flying Machines

Leonardo da Vinci lived more than 500 years ago in Italy. Many people think he was the most clever inventor who ever lived.

Leonardo was a genius. He drew pictures of machines that no one had ever thought of and no one actually built until hundreds of years later. These are some of his wonderful flying machines.

Wings for People

Leonardo drew a **parachute** with a tent-shaped canopy, or top piece. The canopy could catch air and slow the parachute's fall.

He also drew a flying machine that looks like a modern glider!

Helicopter

Leonardo designed a helicopter with a screw mechanism to lift the craft off the ground. It looks modern for the times in which he lived.

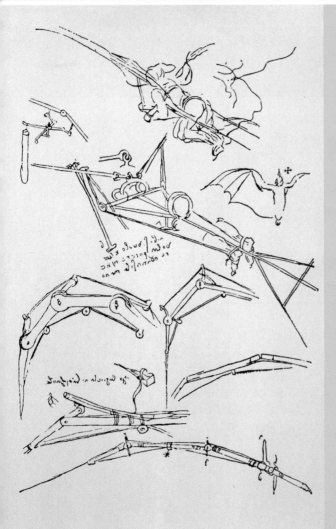

Glider

The glider in this picture has wings that look very much like a bird's wings. Leonardo knew about basic principles of flying, such as **lift** and **aerodynamics**.

Hot Air Balloon

A hot air balloon is another kind of aircraft. It uses hot air to lift off the ground. The first people to fly were carried in the passenger basket of a hot air balloon.

You see hot air balloons today because of us.

Powered by Hot Air

1. The Montgolfier brothers loved the idea of flying. They wanted to fly into the air.

2. They didn't have wings to flap like birds do.

3. They noticed, though, that light objects such as leaves floated in the air.

4. They also saw that smoke rose and floated. So the brothers experimented with smoke-filled bags, making the bags rise.

14

Lifting Off

Hot air is lighter than cold air, so it rises through the colder air around it. When a balloon is filled with hot air, the air inside makes the whole balloon rise. It can pull up a basket that holds passengers.

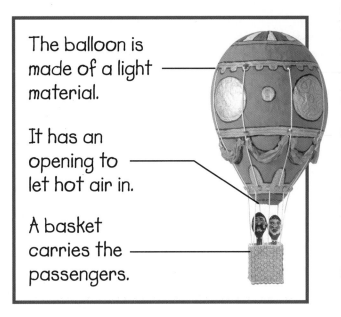

The balloon is made of a light material.

It has an opening to let hot air in.

A basket carries the passengers.

5. They found out that the hot air, not the smoke, is what rose. So they filled bags with hot air and watched the bags take off.

6. Finally they made a huge bag, big enough to carry a basket for passengers. They filled the bag with hot air from a fire, then put a duck, a sheep, and a rooster in the basket. The animals were the first aircraft passengers!

The Airplane

1. The brothers Orville and Wilbur Wright made bicycles, but their real love was flight. They knew hot air made balloons fly. They wanted to invent an aircraft that ran on its own power. They also wanted to control its direction and speed.

2. They knew the wings would be an important part of the machine. They studied the shape of a buzzard's wings.

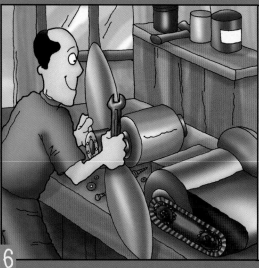

3. They made an engine to drive the blades of a **propeller**. A propeller is like a set of rotating wings. That helped the plane rise through the air.

4. The brothers designed a lightweight aircraft with double wings. The invention worked. In 1903, they tested the first controllable airplane ever invented.

Wing Machine

An airplane is a heavier-than-air aircraft that has wings and is powered by an engine.

The American inventors Orville and Wilbur Wright invented the first airplane. They studied buzzards to see how wings helped birds fly and what shapes worked best. The brothers were determined to start a new era of human flight.

Early planes copied the basic lightweight design of the Wrights' first successful plane.

Controlling Flight

The Wright brothers, and the inventors who came after them, had to perfect planes to make controlled flight easy and safe. Here are some of the improvements.

Controls

The Wrights built airplanes run by propeller engines. They also invented ways to control their craft. They made the airplane nose go up and down with **elevator** flaps. They made **rudders** to turn their air machines left and right.

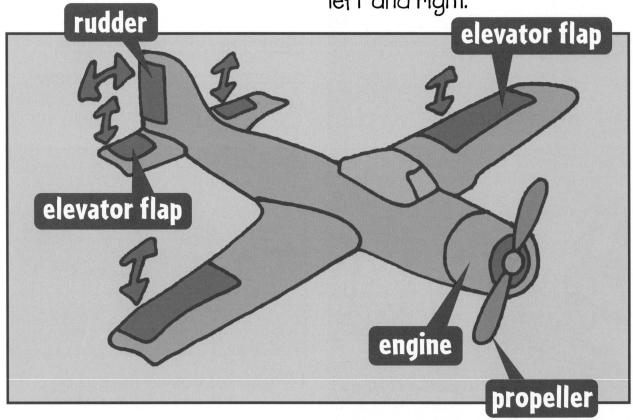

rudder

elevator flap

elevator flap

engine

propeller

Propeller

Propellers act as moving wings, driving a plane forward. The Hawker Hurricane, which came along later, was a fighter plane with a propeller in its nose. Engineers had to make sure its guns didn't shoot the propellers off!

Wheels and Pontoons

Landing a plane would be nearly impossible if it had to skid to a stop. So engineers added wheels to the undercarriage to make landings safer. Some planes were made to land on water. They were built with air-filled tanks, or **pontoons**, on the bottom.

Smooth Shapes

Over the years, propeller-driven aircraft became more streamlined. That means they were given a smooth shape that caused little **friction**.

Planes became faster and safer. The more streamlined a plane is, the faster it will go.

These early planes were called biplanes because they had two wings. They weren't very fast.

Large planes for carrying goods and passengers needed more power, so they had two or sometimes four engines attached to the wings. The first ones weren't very aerodynamic.

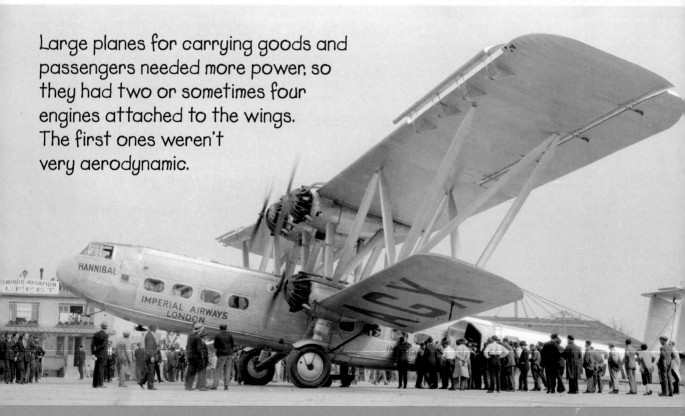

The fighter planes of World War II had smooth lines. They were easier to manage than earlier planes. That ability was handy in dogfights with enemy aircraft.

This Airbus A380 has a smooth aerodynamic shape. It can cruise at very high speeds.

Jet Power

The more pilots flew, the faster they wanted to go. Engineers built bigger propeller engines for more power. Then came another kind of power that engineers used to make planes faster and even sleeker. It was the **jet** engine.

A jet engine doesn't need propellers. Instead, it burns fuel and oxygen in a compartment in the engine. The burning makes hot gas shoot from the back of the engine. That pushes the craft forward in the opposite direction.

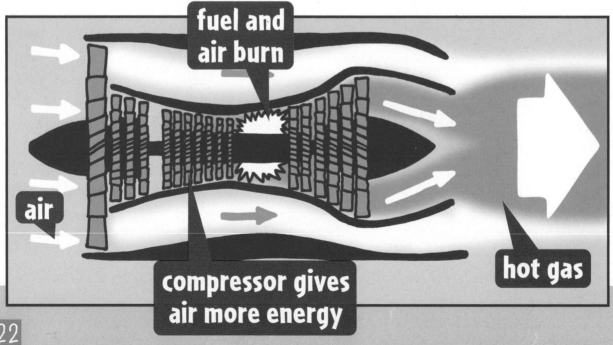

fuel and air burn

air

compressor gives air more energy

hot gas

Jets can travel faster than the speed of sound. The speed of sound is 660 miles (1,062 kilometers) per hour at a height of 20,000 feet (6,096 meters).

Fighter Planes

Perhaps the most exciting aircraft to see and hear are the ones used for fighting. They're fast, sleek, and noisy.

Lancaster Bomber ▲

Pilots flew Lancasters during World War II. The Lancaster bombers had **gun turrets**. Crews of gunners could fire at attacking fighters.

Fokker Triplane ▲

The Fokker triplane was flown in World War I. It carried two machine guns and could fly 124 miles (200 kilometers) per hour.

Hawker Hurricane

The Hurricane was used to shoot down German bombers during the Battle of Britain in 1940. The guns were fixed so that pilots could fly closer to their targets than was previously considered safe. ◄

Hawker Hurricane

Sabre

The U.S. jet the Sabre was one of the first jet fighters ever built.

B-52 Bomber ▶

The B-52 bomber was flown during the Vietnam War, but it's still being used today.

Blackbird

The Lockheed SR-71 Blackbird set a world speed record of 2,193 miles (3,529 kilometers) per hour in 1976.

◀

The Helicopter

Airplanes are great for flying, but they need long runways to land. The Russian inventor Igor Sikorsky thought it would be a good idea to invent an aircraft that could take off and land vertically. So he invented the helicopter.

Leonardo da Vinci designed a helicopter long before Sikorsky, but it was never built.

Igor Sikorsky flies his first helicopter.

VTOL

A helicopter is a **VTOL** craft. That stands for vertical takeoff and landing. The blades of the craft turn quickly, making the air above move very quickly. That lowers that air's pressure. The turning blades act as wings do, making the higher air pressure below push the helicopter up from underneath.

Go-Everywhere Machines

Helicopters can fly forward, backward, and hover in the air. They can get to the places airplanes can't reach. Helicopters are used to carry soldiers from place to place and to protect soldiers from above. These aircraft can also rescue people from remote and dangerous places.

The Rocket

After pilots started conquering the air, they began looking beyond it. To get to outer space, they would need something really powerful: a **rocket**!

A rocket is a flying machine powered by exploding gases. It uses fuel, such as **nitrogen**, mixed with oxygen. The fuel can be in solid or liquid form. When the fuel and oxygen are mixed and ignited, they expand, or grow larger, fast. That creates a huge force, an explosion that pushes the rocket forward. The push is the rocket's **thrust**.

1. Scientists wanted to build a craft that could fly to the moon. They needed huge amounts of fuel to power the craft away from Earth.

2. The fuel needed to explode, creating expanding gas that could thrust the rocket upward.

A Controlled Explosion

3. In 1926, a scientist named Robert Goddard designed the first liquid-fuel rocket, but it was small.

4. In 1932, he made a larger rocket with fins and controls for stability. It didn't go very far—just 197 feet (60 meters). Yet it was a start!

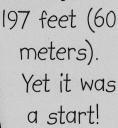

5. By 1969, rockets had powered astronauts to the Moon and back.

Flight Quiz

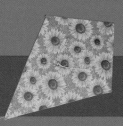

1. What kind of engine powers a modern jet fighter?

2. Which part moves up and down to help a plane go up and down?

3. Which type of aircraft can fly forward, backward, and hover in the air?

4. Which inventor was the first to draw a helicopter?

5. What do we call the weight of air that presses down on us?

6. What part of a plane creates lift when in the air?

7. Why can a hot air balloon fly?

8. Who invented the controllable airplane?

9. Which aircraft broke the world air speed record in 1976?

10. What mixture explodes to power a rocket into space?

1. Jet engine 2. Elevator flap 3. Helicopter 4. Leonardo da Vinci 5. Air pressure 6. The wings 7. Hot air is lighter than cold air 8. The Wright brothers 9. The Blackbird 10. Fuel and oxygen

Glossary

aerodynamics: the study of how air moves around objects

elevator flaps: flaps that move up and down to help a plane move correctly

friction: a rubbing which can act to slow down the objects that rub

glider: an aircraft that rides on airflow for short flight without an engine

gun turrets: flat armored towers used to house guns and gunners

hover: to remain floating or flying in nearly the same place in the air

jet: an airplane powered by engines that create a stream of gas

lift: a force created by air moving past a wing and related air pressure changes

molecules: the smallest particles of a thing having characteristics of that thing

nitrogen: a gas that can be mixed with oxygen and ignited to push rockets

parachute: an umbrella-like cloth that can catch wind to slow a fall

pontoons: the hollow floats used to keep craft on top of the water

propeller: a blade that spins with others to drive craft through air or water

rocket: an aircraft powered by the igniting and explosion of oxygen and fuels

rudders: the flat, moving pieces positioned at the back of craft to aid steering

streamlined: having a shape that gets through air or water easily

thrust: the driving force of a propeller, a jet, or a rocket

VTOL: the ability to go straight up or down, for (v)ertical (t)ake(o)ff and (l)anding

Index